THE WHITE CROW (EICHMANN IN JERUSALEM)

Donald Freed

BROADWAY PLAY PUBLISHING INC
224 E 62nd St, NY, NY 10065
www.broadwayplaypub.com
info@broadwayplaypub.com

THE WHITE CROW
© Copyright 2003 by Donald Freed

This play was originally published by B P P I in September 2003 in the collection *Plays By Donald Freed, Volume Two*

First printing of this edition: November 2010
I S B N: 978-0-88145-471-0

Book design: Marie Donovan
Typographic controls & page make-up: Adobe InDesign
Typeface: Palatino
Printed and bound in the U S A

"Donald Freed is a writer of blazing imagination, courage, and insight. His work is a unique and fearless marriage of politics and wit."
Harold Pinter

THE WHITE was recently produced by York Theatre Royal from 1-23 May 2009. The cast and creative contributors were:

EICHMANN .... Robert Pickavance
DR BAUM .... Sonia Petrovna
GUARD .... Christopher Bewers

Director .... Damian Cruden
Design .... Lydia Denno
Sound design .... Craig Vear

CHARACTERS & SETTING

Adolph Eichmann
Miriam Baum
Guard

Time: summer, 1960

Place: Jerusalem

AUTHOR'S NOTE

Adolph Karl Eichmann, the Nazi war criminal captive, is confronted by the Israeli psychologist Doctor Miriam Baum. The setting is the basement of a police building in Isreal. There is one small window.

The character of Doctor Baum is a fictional creation based on fact. Eichmann is an historical personage, re-imagined at the level of drama. The third character is an Isreali orderly.

The interrogation room has a table, chairs, chalkboard, two tape recorders, and piles of documents in every corner.

ACT ONE

(ADOLPH EICHMANN, *blind-folded, is marched in by an armed guard. Left alone, he removes the blindfold and stares about him. Then, he scurries about the room gathering and checking on his "evidence". Without his glasses, he is like a frantic mole. He has also been deprived of his belt and shoelaces, so he must hold up his trousers at crucial moments of action.)*

(The plain, official room contains a table, chairs, a white-board and marker—and mounds of documents. A fan turns overhead. There are two tape recorders at one side of the room; one for recording the interview and the other for pre-recorded use. There is a barred window on one wall. There is also a tray with a container of water and two glasses.)

(A GUARD *is heard unlocking elaborate safeguards outside the door.* EICHMANN *leaps to rigid attention as the door opens and a* GUARD *enters, followed by a middle-aged woman in uniform,* MIRIAM BAUM.*)*

*(*BAUM *carries a legal briefcase, from which she will draw documents throughout the play. The* GUARD *hangs a huge photograph of Auschwitz on the wall.* EICHMANN *thinks the* GUARD *is in charge, because he is male.* EICHMANN *mistakenly addresses the guard.)*

EICHMANN: At your orders, sir! Permit me, your honor, to express my appreciation for the flawless coordination, and ah, special... *(He stutters in confusion at the* GUARD's *exit.)*

BAUM: *(The two study each other after she circles the room.)* Good morning, Colonel. I am Doctor Baum. Serving temporarily on special assignment with Bureau 06 of the police of the State of Israel.

EICHMANN: At your service, Frau-Captain-Professor-Doctor Baum.

BAUM: Colonel, I am informed that you are ready and willing to give us, in preparation for your trial, a complete version of your role in the special activities of Section IV B 4 of the Third Reich.

EICHMANN: As God is my witness. *(He has recovered his Prussian style, mixed with a certain Austrian "charm".)*

BAUM: Please be at ease. Sit down. No, please...I *insist*! I've been informed that you have expressed a need for certain additional maps and documents. I've brought some with me and others will be made available to you as we locate them. *(Turns on the tape machine)* Now, sir, our conversation will be recorded here on tape.

EICHMANN: Permit me, Doctor, to remark that it is a pleasure to listen to a perfect German such as yours, after many years of South-American-style Spanish.

BAUM: Thank you. Now, I have to inform you, sir, that these interviews must be conducted in English.

EICHMANN: In English, Your Honor?

BAUM: Yes, sir, it is, ah, a diplomatic decision.

EICHMANN: I see. At your service. English, German, Spanish: it's either true or it isn't.

BAUM: Quite... Your flight from Argentina was, ah, comfortable? And your quarters are satisfactory?

EICHMANN: *Ja.* A little large, but I feel at home.

BAUM: You had a meal last night?

EICHMANN: *Ja*, something "mid-Eastern," but you know, I prefer the, uh, German Kosher style, professor.

(BAUM *leans back and looks at* EICHMANN.)

BAUM: ...But you are feeling well? After the shock of your arrest?

EICHMANN: *Ja*, it was like a bolt from the blue—but now I'm fit as a fiddle.

BAUM: Good. Then you slept well last night?

EICHMANN: Well—the first few nights, you know.... Uh, pardon me, Your Honor, but I was led to believe that Chief Prosecutor Hausner was to personally handle my case.

BAUM: I am assigned to you for today only, sir.

(Pause)

EICHMANN: I am delighted, of course.... Now, Professor, we come to the matter of my glasses.

BAUM: Yes. Here they are.

EICHMANN: *(Seeing the photograph)* What is that?

BAUM: I beg your pardon? Your request, here, read. Quote: "One early photograph from Auschwitz." Close quotes. Here, please look at the document, Colonel.

EICHMANN: ...What a comedy, Your Honor. What I wrote was— "One *aerial* photograph *of* Auschwitz." Oh, dear, dear. A-ha.

BAUM: I see. And why did you require it?

EICHMANN: To indicate the distance from the depot to the, uh...

BAUM: I see. Well, let me turn it to the wall and we'll forget about it. So sorry, a misunderstanding...

EICHMANN: *Ja, ja*... And the belt and—

BAUM: Plastic lenses for your spectacles are being made—until then you may wear your regular spectacles in this room under supervision.

EICHMANN: Of course, you are under orders—

BAUM: Precisely. *(Pause)* Now, the guards rotate tasting your rations, so that—

EICHMANN: *Ja.* They are fine young men, but not a one speaks either German or Spanish.

BAUM: No.

EICHMANN: Or even Yiddish... You were raised in Germany?

BAUM: I got out in 1939, to England.

EICHMANN: Thank God...and your family? *(Pause)* You don't look...German.

BAUM: No? Can you tell me the German look?

EICHMANN: At your service. *(Clicks heels, smiles, and proceeds to describe himself.)* Example: big ears, hook nose, stigmatism, bald head, flat feet, hernia: in short, Doctor—the Superman.

(EICHMANN *laughs*, BAUM *does not.*)

BAUM: *Ja...* Umm, for your own protection, you are the sole prisoner in this complex, and its whereabouts have not been made public. You are blindfolded in order to—

EICHMANN: Please do not concern yourself, Captain, I intend to make my appearance at the trial. There is much that must be said....

BAUM: Yes.

EICHMANN: That has not been said.

BAUM: Yes. You have been given periodicals and books for your reading. Is this satisfactory?

EICHMANN: I have, of course, had no time, Professor.
However, I note that one of the books, Lolita....

BAUM: Yes.

EICHMANN: I mean it's, ah, an unwholesome, uh, it's
filth.... Why was it supplied to me? ...But I have read
this morning's newspaper, I believe it is the organ
of the Isreali Communist Party. It points out that,
quote, "...it is simply breathtaking that the prosecution
of Eichmann will accuse him of complicity in the
infamous Nuremberg race laws when, thanks to the
orthodox rabbinical laws of Isreal, a person born of a
non-Jewish mother can neither be married nor buried."
Close quotes.

BAUM: We have a free press here, Colonel.

EICHMANN: Wonderful, Doctor. Professor. Please, do
not misunderstand. I have waited fourteen years for
this opportunity. I mean no disrespect, please.... Mmm,
one thing.

BAUM: Yes.

EICHMANN: A violin. If I might—

BAUM: Yes, I know, I understand you are rather good
and I am in favor of it. However—

EICHMANN: I mean, I would not cut my throat with the
bow.

BAUM: No, but the decision is rather...

(EICHMANN *clicks his heels again, pantomimes playing,
making the sound with his voice.* BAUM *stares at him.*)

EICHMANN: Brahms, you know, Your Honor.

(BAUM *stares, hard-eyed.*)

BAUM: Now, it is my assignment, today only, to review
a few elementary facts, and then cede to experts on the

"Final Solution," who will begin their interrogations next week.

EICHMANN: Experts, Doctor?

BAUM: Yes. Men from: Austria, the "Protectorate"; France; Belgium; The Netherlands; Norway; Denmark; Italy; Yugoslavia; Bulgaria; Romania; Hungary; Slovakia; Finland; and Germany. —No rush; the trial cannot commence until late next year, so....

EICHMANN: I see. And you...

BAUM: I will be out of the country, at that time....

EICHMANN: Experts. *Ja, ja,* I know all about experts. I *was* one. Later we call experts "war criminals." Forgive my gallows humor, Doctor, but I believe it is permitted since we both know that no matter what I say or do here, the verdict will be "Guilty as Charged."

BAUM: Is that how you see the trial, Colonel? What do you imagine that "they" have in store for you?

EICHMANN: Well, I mean Albert Speer, himself—the Fuhrer's favorite—only got twenty years. And he was, uh—and, I mean, I am only, I was only, uh... I mean, perhaps five years or, at the most, uh.... *Ja.* But, of course, Speer was tried at Nuremberg by an international court. And I am here in Jerusalem.

BAUM: I have nothing to do with the trial itself. I am here for today only.

(*A long pause as the idea of the possible death sentence sinks in on* EICHMANN.)

EICHMANN: You have nothing to do with the trial?

BAUM: No, sir.

EICHMANN: What are you orders, then, sir?

BAUM: As I have told you. —Orientation, ah, general background, ah, for the "record," you know.

EICHMANN: *Ja.* The record.

BAUM: For instance, we have very little material on your whereabouts after the German defeat in 1945, in fact until your apprehension last week in Buenos Aires.

EICHMANN: Nothing out of the ordinary—

BAUM: *(Overlapping)* How you escaped Germany. How you found a new life in Latin—

EICHMANN: I walked away! *Ja*— Until I was "invented" as a scapegoat at Nuremberg, nobody knew Adolph Eichmann from Adam. I walked away. Like a bit player...

BAUM: You walked away? —How can this be?

EICHMANN: Doctor—when the circus is over, the clowns change clothes and stretch their legs. Does anyone recognize them?

(BAUM and EICHMANN stare at each other. He smiles slowly. She makes a note.)

BAUM: Ja...Now, I believe that we should begin with just a few basic facts... *(She checks the tape machine.)* You were born....

EICHMANN: I was born...

(BAUM and EICHMANN's eyes meet. He raises his voice.)

EICHMANN: ...in the Rhineland...

BAUM: No need to strain, the microphones are placed so that—

EICHMANN: In the Rhineland.

BAUM: May 10, 1906?

EICHMANN: *Ja.*

BAUM: Your father's names was—

EICHMANN: Adolph Karl. My mother's name was Maria....

BAUM: Were you religiously affiliated?

EICHMANN: As a youth, I belonged to the Evangelical Church. My father was very religious.

BAUM: Do you still believe in God?

EICHMANN: *(Reacting sharply)* Of course...in my own way...

BAUM: You attended the Kaiser Franz State School? I'm reading from the statement you prepared in Buenos Aires.

EICHMANN: Yes, sir.

BAUM: You know, of course, that some fifteen years earlier, Adoph Hitler attended that same school?

EICHMANN: Yes, sir.

BAUM: Curious...you don't mention it in your statement. Have you changed your attitude toward—

EICHMANN: I have changed my attitude toward many things.

BAUM: Perhaps, later, we may touch on the subject of the Fuhrer.

EICHMANN: At your service.

(BAUM *notices a malfunction of the tape recorder.* EICHMANN *immediately crouches and begins to tinker and tamper. He hums and chats—in his element. She studies him, at her feet, as he works.)*

EICHMANN: Please allow me, please, no force needed. No force. Hmm... Aha... *Ja*... The Japs, you know, they.... *Ja, ja*—that does it, my doctor. *(He smiles happily up at her.)*

BAUM: Thank you, sir. You are quite, ah—

EICHMANN: *Ja*, ja, handy. My father always said to me: "Trust your hands."

BAUM: Your father, later, went into his own business?

EICHMANN: *Ja*. He bought an interest in a Locomobile outlet. Then the slump... He failed—every penny. His partner hung himself in the tool shed.

(EICHMANN *is still crouched at* BAUM's *feet. Both are becoming self-conscious.*)

BAUM: Your relationship with your father was—

EICHMANN: Perfect.

BAUM: *Ja*. And your relationship with your own sons is, you would say—

EICHMANN: The same.

BAUM: With all four? Dieter, Klaus, Horst...?

EICHMANN: *Ja*.

BAUM: And you have a little one—Riccardo Francisco.

EICHMANN: *Ja*. We call him "Haasi"...

BAUM: And what is he like?

EICHMANN: An angel... Do you, yourself, have children, Doctor?

BAUM: Please get up, sir, and we can then—

EICHMANN: You seem so fascinated with my personal life.... Do you have any of your own?

BAUM: We are here, sir, to look at *your* life. It is not a question of "personal" or "public". Simply a life—yours.

EICHMANN: So? And yours?

BAUM: My life, Colonel, is of no interest whatsoever. Surely, you see that goes beyond our guidelines.

(EICHMANN *clicks his heels, then retreats to his documents.* BAUM *checks the tape.*)

BAUM: ...Would you care for a cigarette? Go on... Your schooling was....

EICHMANN: *(He smokes with gusto.)* Thank you, Your Honor. Ahh, a Zippo...School? *Ja*, I left school. My first job was—salesman for Gargoyl Gasoline and Vacuum Oil. I was ordered to set up gas stations in all of upper Austria.

BAUM: You stayed with them through—

EICHMANN: *Ja*, this was for *me*! That part of Austria is a hundred years behind the time, with old-fashioned people and places—I love it. Do you know it?

BAUM: *Ja*, very old-fashioned.

EICHMANN: *Ja*, you know it! *(He is rapturous.)*

BAUM: I spent three months of my *wanderjahr* walking from Innsbruck to Grosslochner, through the towns around the Gruehn Wald—the Wildsitze.

EICHMANN: The Zugspitze; the Raab and the Rhine. This was my youth—the evergreen forests, the valleys between—

BAUM: *Ja*, the old castles.

EICHMANN: The ruined gentry, pure romance! ...If the company hadn't transferred me without warning to Salzburg, I'd be there still.... But, they let me go because I was the only unmarried salesman.... You look so...do I know you from somewhere?

BAUM: This was 1933? Then you went to Germany. Was there a problem at home?

EICHMANN: *(Nervous)* Perhaps—

BAUM: You say here, that—

EICHMANN: *Financial.* —Anyway I left.

BAUM: Were you "political" by this time?

EICHMANN: As schoolboys we were all revolutionaries and monarchists.... *Ja.* Our mottoes were: "A Clean Mind in a Clean Body," and "Public Need Before Private Greed"... *(He hums and sways to an old school anthem. She studies him.)* Then, that was when a certain Ernst Kaltenbrunner came to our town fair—and said to me, man to man: "I've had my eye on you. You have something. Why not join the S S?"

BAUM: And you replied?

EICHMANN: "Why not?"

(Pause, she studies him.)

BAUM: The year?

EICHMANN: *(Piercing sadness)* 1933... My new uniform was bought and paid for. It was at the tailor's waiting for me.... *(A deep sigh)* Then out of the blue the authorities suppressed the Party in Austria. So that is why I decided to leave for Germany.

BAUM: And you reported to the S A Army camp at Lechfield?

EICHMANN: *Ja, ja,* I had to leave my red motorbike behind, too.

BAUM: What were your impressions of this period?

EICHMANN: My impressions? ...The doctor selected me for the shock troops, the special police (I was not then the wreck you see before you, now), and we were trained for street fighting. It's all thick forest there, like my home, where I was... *(He stares at the turning tape.)*

BAUM: Would you like some water? We will have the luncheon recess quite soon. And, of course, tea later.

EICHMANN: *(Suddenly flaring up)* I understood that Mister Ben-Gurion would be sending Chief Prosecutor Hausner in person to see me.

BAUM: Mr Hausner is not in Jerusalem at the moment.

EICHMANN: But I was distinctly told he would be—

BAUM: He will be, Colonel Eichmann! You were speaking of Lechfield...the barracks at Lechfield.

EICHMANN: *(Pause, then regaining his poise)* At your service! *Ja*—hot sausages, pancakes, and the barracks life. It passed like a dream; then before Christmas we were all sent for further training to Dachau. There, it was a different story. There, we learned real discipline. Horses! There, the S S wore the death's-head on their collars: my eyes were like saucers.

BAUM: I'm not clear how you passed from Dachau to Himmler's staff.

EICHMANN: Doctor, believe me when I tell you it was a comedy of errors. First, I was in my element at Dachau. I worked like a dog and was promoted right along. So when I heard that there were openings in Himmler's secret service, naturally I stepped forward. But you see I had misunderstood: I believed that Himmler's "Security" would get to ride around on the running boards of the General's cars, like bodyguards in the movies with guns drawn! That was my mental picture. *(He mimes his image.)*

BAUM: Instead—

EICHMANN: Instead, they listed me as "unmarried, therefore single", and shipped me off to the Palace on the Wilhemstrasse, where I promptly slipped on the parquet floor and bruised my spine. My desk was in the bowels of the building. Every day I had to pass by coffins with bones and magical signs glowing in the dark. It was a nightmare. They told me that I was in the Free Masonry Museum. My doctor, I couldn't even pronounce the name "Free Masonry" —all I had wanted was to ride around on the running boards with the guns drawn....

BAUM: Like in the movies. And then one day you were "promoted" upstairs to meet Captain von Mildenstein?

EICHMANN: *Ja.* And Captain von Mildenstein remarked that he was in the process of organizing a "Jews Department" somewhere, and would I be at all interested.

BAUM: What was the official title of this section?

EICHMANN: "Jews."

BAUM: Ah.

EICHMANN: That's it. Captain von Mildenstein was my superior. A wonderful man, a civilized human being. The first thing he did was give me Theodore Herzl's The Jewish State.

BAUM: Did you read it?

EICHMANN: A classic. Many times. My eyes were opened. A new state! I was deeply moved! It made a lasting impression.

(EICHMANN *stares at the turning tape as* BAUM *stares at him. Pause. She smashes an insect on the table. He reacts.*)

BAUM: A spider... You're very apprehensive, aren't you, sir?

EICHMANN: No, sir.

BAUM: Your passage from Argentina was rather—

EICHMANN: Not at all. Your secret police wrapped me up in blankets, in a wheel chair, with dark glasses— and announced that I was an old man returning to Jerusalem to die. Like the wandering Jew searching the world for his grave.

(*Pause*)

BAUM: *Ja.* Let's see: In 1939, you were sent to meet with Zionist leaders in the Middle East, weren't you? (*Pause*) Have a cigarette.

EICHMANN: *(He ducks his head obsequiously and takes one.)* Please. Thank you, Your Honor. *Ja,* I had two stars by then and I knew the top Zionists, and I agreed one hundred percent with their position. I wanted to send as many Jews as possible from Germany to Palestine... This was what our office wanted, this is what the Zionists wanted. We were one and the same.

BAUM: You refer in your summary to the "mutual advantages" to both Germans and Jews of your various plans for emigration. Is that correct?

EICHMANN: Yes, sir.

BAUM: *(Handing over documents)* Yet, here we see, and you know, that laws were passed by this time, by 1937, that extracted huge fines from Jews: billions.

EICHMANN: *Ja,* Doctor, strictly speaking, they were forced to emigrate. But I had no part in these laws, of course. We were stuck away reading books in our lazy, quiet cubbyhole of an office.

(EICHMANN leans over the table. BAUMe leans over to face him.)

BAUM: Quite. Now, sir, we are reaching the critical turning point—1939—and I want to try to understand how your quiet, lazy little office became the eye of the hurricane—of the Holocaust.

EICHMANN: *Ja, ja...*We are a good team. At this rate, we can finish by the luncheon hour.... Your Honor has places she would rather be...no? *Jetzt moechten Sie Mittagesen.*

BAUM: *Wir essen um zu leben.* We eat to live. But we have our work to do.

EICHMANN: Exactly. I mean, you would not spend one minute in my company unless you were ordered to.

BAUM: I don't take your point, Colonel.

EICHMANN: Orders, Captain. You are here under orders. No other reason. Orders. Your orders. *Ja, ja.*

(BAUM *and* EICHMANN *stare at each other; an invisible boundary has been crossed.*)

BAUM: That is true. I have my orders. And I have my reasons. *Befehle.*

EICHMANN: *Befehle.* Fated, Doctor...

BAUM: *Ja, ja*...well...

EICHMANN: I'm told that, today, German youth is suffering from a guilt complex because of these events!

BAUM: So?

EICHMANN: So, that is why I am here, Captain, and raise no objections to the events in the Argentine attendant on my "arrest." I am here to speak the God's truth and to write it all down—if you will give me time—so that my sons and all of German youth can once again hold up its head. So, fire away!

BAUM: Hitler's *Mein Kampf* was your Bible, correct?

EICHMANN: No, Doctor.

BAUM: No?

EICHMANN: I never read it.... A few pages maybe—

BAUM: But those few pages put you in the picture as to what was to happen?

EICHMANN: Absolutely not!

BAUM: Did you read this? Quote: "We are passing a magnet over a dunghill.... Under its pressure so-called `humanity'—that mixture of stupidity, cowardice, and imaginary intelligence—will melt like snow from the March sun.... The Jew will disappear from Europe..."

EICHMANN: I don't know it.

BAUM: Or this: "Conscience is a Jewish invention."

EICHMANN: Fantastic!

BAUM: "If a people is to become free, it needs pride and willpower, defiance, hate, hate and once again hate."

EICHMANN: *(He echoes her quote.)* "...Hate." That I remember. When he spoke...some time, we must discuss that, Your Honor.

(Pause)

BAUM: You attended the same school. You shared the same general orientation.... You were both Austro-Germans, weren't you?

EICHMANN: And there, the resemblance ended, believe me.

BAUM: I see. You were an "individual".

EICHMANN: Exactly, Professor, one man. Just one ordinary man.

(BAUM pauses, smokes, walks to the auxiliary tape machine.)

BAUM: Mm... Do you remember Nuremberg, 1936?

(BAUM pushes the button. The Sieg Heils! bounce off the concrete walls of the interrogation room. Then, she lowers the volume to a dull roar. EICHMANN stands next to her.)

BAUM: So many.

EICHMANN: *Ja.*

BAUM: You were there.

EICHMANN: Of course.

BAUM: Can you hear yourself in the, ah, crowd?

(EICHMANN looks at BAUM, then shakes his head. She turns the sound off.)

EICHMANN: You don't believe me. You think I'm hiding something, don't you?

BAUM: Yes... But not from me so much as from yourself...

EICHMANN: Then mesmerize me. Who are you really? Are you a hypnotist? Go on, I'm not afraid.

(BAUM *studies* EICHMANN, *then smiles and shrugs.*)

BAUM: If it were so easy...I think we must just press on.

EICHMANN: *Ja, ja.*

BAUM: You knew the Party program?

EICHMANN: The twelve points?

BAUM: The twenty-five points... Points denying all rights to Jews.

EICHMANN: *(Overlapping)* No one took them seriously. Doctor, National Socialism was a "movement", not a "Party". The "points" were for, you know, to appeal to the old-fashioned bourgeois voters—

BAUM: And the Jews, themselves, actually were "old-fashioned" enough to believe in "legality," isn't that true?

EICHMANN: *Ja,* but, Doctor, Professor, as far as the order to expel Jews across borders—I must tell you that it hit our office like a thunderclap.

BAUM: *(Boring in)* March, 1938: the Anschluss.

EICHMANN: I was sent back to Vienna overnight!

BAUM: *(Overlapping)* Your whole career hung in the balance.

EICHMANN: I was frantic—

BAUM: And your success was *spectacular*: in eight months fifty percent of Austria's Jewry was driven out. You "cleansed" Austria "legally".

(BAUM *and* EICHMANN *each reaches for documents as they need them in the next section.*)

EICHMANN: You say *I*, doctor. I never dreamed what was coming. Even as late as the *morning* of

Kristallnacht—the *morning*—do you know what
Heydrich said? "The "problem' is not to make the rich
Jews leave, but only to get rid of the Jewish mob."

BAUM: The riff-raff?

EICHMANN: That's what they wanted in Berlin.

BAUM: And what did they want in Vienna? *(Pause)*
Vienna was an assembly line wasn't it? At one end you
put in a Jew who still had some property—a shop, a
bank account—and he comes out at the other end with
only a passport and two weeks to leave the country or
go to a concentration camp. Correct, Colonel?

EICHMANN: Yes, doctor. But we must appreciate that
within the frame-work of possibilities, I felt we were
doing justice to both parties—

BAUM: So you have written here—

EICHMANN: *(Overlapping)* Because the Jews desired to
emigrate, and Germany, for her part—

BAUM: *(Erupting and recovering)* But, Colonel, sir, *why*
did they "*desire*" to emigrate? ...Never mind, we are
getting too far afield.... You were ordered to take
charge of "Jewish affairs", and you did?

EICHMANN: Like any good functionary, I threw myself
into the job.

BAUM: Why? Why did everyone say that you were so
intense, so fanatically eager to—

EICHMANN: *(Overlapping)* My Doctor, when you are
in uniform, there is only one way to carry out orders.
Cowards in the dock at Nuremberg may call this
"fanaticism", but ask any Army man—ask those fine
and frightening young men in the corridor standing
guard. They are under orders and they will do as you
say.

BAUM: Yes, and four years ago when an Israeli patrol—under *orders*—fired on Arab women and children, they were court-martialled.

EICHMANN: I'm only human. I obeyed. I obeyed all orders. I obeyed, I obeyed! Do you want chaos?

BAUM: If for instance, a superior gives an order to shoot civilians— "Shoot them!" —must the subordinate obey?

EICHMANN: Absolutely. Even as your early Zionists massacred Palestinian peasants. Do you want anarchy?

BAUM: But you knew that your orders were illegal!

EICHMANN: Doctor, if they had said to me, "Your father is a traitor— kill him!" —I would have done it.

BAUM: Your father?

EICHMANN: *Ja!* We were surrounded by death.... Today's youth can never understand... But I could have said "no"...hmmm? That's what you want me to say, isn't it, Doctor?

(Pause)

BAUM: I want you to tell me the facts. That's all.

EICHMANN: Here is the point, Doctor: I personally committed no act of violence, and was not ordered to. —You look stunned. I tell you that I never ordered the death of a Jew, or of any human being. *(Like a machine)* Nevertheless, I did abide by Section 11: I did my "best to reduce the gravity of the consequences of the offense..." Uh, it's in the record somewhere.

BAUM: You did this?

EICHMANN: Absolutely, Doctor.

BAUM: When?

EICHMANN: Until the end.

BAUM: Where?

EICHMANN: Vienna, Prague—I bent over backwards.

BAUM: What do you mean?

EICHMANN: It's in the record!: In Vienna, in the excitement, I slapped the Jewish leader, Doctor Lowenberg, for complaining too much about the situation of the Jews. But I apologized immediately—in full uniform—in front of my staff. In my department, I did not permit physical violence. *(He clicks his heels.)*

BAUM: You have a great flair, sir. But I do not follow your logic in terms of illegal orders.

EICHMANN: *(He spits out his credo.)* Pardon me, Professor, Doctor, there were no "illegal" orders or "legal" orders. There were only *orders*. Full stop. Orders! Permit me, I will try to be calm. Forgive me...Doctor Lowenberg, you know, he and I, the Jewish leadership itself—worked hand in hand in the "Reorganization of Jewish Life" in Vienna—

BAUM: One moment, please. Why did they work "hand in hand," and where was the justification for this "reorganization" of Jewish life—

EICHMANN: There is none—

BAUM: *(Overlapping)* —In Vienna—

EICHMANN: *(Overlapping)* —And I would never have ordered it—

BAUM: *(Her voice rising)* —Which led, in the end, to the ovens and the tank ditches!

EICHMANN: Doctor Lowenberg and I tried—

BAUM: *(Overlapping. She explodes, recovers.)* Excuse me, Colonel! ...I'm afraid if we both speak at once, the stenographer will be unable—

(BAUM *and* EICHMANN *breathe and study each other.*)

EICHMANN: Of course. Forgive me, Captain...

BAUM: Water?

EICHMANN: *(Takes water)* ...Who are you?

BAUM: Pardon?

EICHMANN: Do you have something, ah, personal against me? ...Do I know you?

BAUM: Do you? *(Pause)* So—in Austria, you organized the forced exit of the entire Jewish population. This was unheard of in modern history.

EICHMANN: *Ja*, modern history. But not in "our" Old Testament: "And the Lord God of Israel smote the tribe of" —somebody or other— "and they were no more." In the land of Goshen. It's in the Bible.

BAUM: Are you now raising the question of the Ammorites, in your defense, Colonel?

EICHMANN: I have no "defense", Doctor. The charges against me, from Nuremberg, are vaudeville! Not even Hitler could have been proved legally guilty.

BAUM: Why is that?

EICHMANN: Because there are no documents linking him to the "Final Solution", much less me. And yet I take responsibility.

BAUM: *Legal* responsibility?

EICHMANN: No. I am legally innocent.

BAUM: And why is that?

EICHMANN: I was one man—with no power. Someone pushed a button in Berlin and a "conveyor belt" began to move in Vienna. Everyone tried to exploit the situation: lawyers who had to accompany the Jews for a fat fee; "organizers" ready to swoop down on Jewish businesses. Everyone was suddenly a "Jewish Expert." Strutting, mouthing grand phrases, profiteering— while I never took a penny! I was the only one who

never made a profit from all of it. And I helped as
many as I could!

BAUM: You did? Can you name one case?

EICHMANN: Of course...the millionaire, Kleiner. I
intervened in his behalf.

BAUM: In what way?

EICHMANN: He was sent to Auschwitz, by mistake. I
intervened so that he was granted permission to sit
down every four hours. He said that the labor was
killing him.

BAUM: Do you know what became of him?

EICHMANN: Kleiner? The next time I got back from
Hungary, I heard that Kleiner had been shot... (*A deep
sigh*)

BAUM: There were eighty million good Germans, each
of whom had his decent Jew. Kleiner was your "decent
Jew", is that it?

(EICHMANN *begins to pace.*)

BAUM: Have I upset you?

EICHMANN: I was lost the day I swore my oath. On
that day, I, too, became a victim of what you call the
"Holocaust". Today no man, no judge in the world
will ever be capable of forcing me to swear an oath, I
will hang myself in public in order that the German
youth of today can understand how we swore away
our souls—and yet, I swear to you that my dream was
to find a place where the Israelite people could live
and have firm ground under their feet. I myself was a
Christian Zionist. A fanatic! I was prepared to empty
convents to make room for Zionist settlers. This was
my dream.

BAUM: Tell me about this dream. (*His dream pours out as
he grabs for documents.*)

EICHMANN: I studied the "basic books" of Judaism and I drew my inspiration from them: First, came the idea of "Nisko". It was 1939, Poland was partitioned with Russia and my idea—and Heydrich agreed—was to set up an autonomous state in our section of Poland. The Nisko section—

BAUM: But what about the millions of Poles already living there?

EICHMANN: Ah, ha! Dear Doctor, I said, "Let the Poles, for once, be moved out and make way for the Jews!" Everything looked marvelous for the Nisko plan until Berlin said, "no". And the whole thing went kaput.

BAUM: Did you then say to Berlin— "Well, this plan of yours is criminal," and resign your office?

EICHMANN: *(Overlapping)* No, you see I was an idealist! I marched right back with the "Madagascar Plan"! And it would have worked! Four million to Madagascar would have—

BAUM: Left more than two million Jews in Poland alone.

EICHMANN: Well, in '38 —no, I mean to say 1939, uh—

BAUM: You mean the extermination of three million Polish Jews was already underway, leaving four million for Madagascar? Colonel, Madagascar was merely a screen behind which to implement preparations for the "Final Solution", was it not?

EICHMANN: I appeal to God in Heaven if I, at least, did not believe in the Madagascar plan! Or, later, Palestine, but there, of course, the British were more fanatical than we were. They *invented* the concentration camp. The British starved them on ships waiting to be admitted; they, they—

BAUM: *(Overlapping)* These were *your* three "dreams"?

EICHMANN: These were my three dreams, Doctor:
Nisko, Madagascar, Palestine. Then out of nowhere
came the war against Russia, and my career was over,
like that.

BAUM: Yet you were promoted three whole grades in
less than eighteen—

EICHMANN: Pardon me, sir, I mean all hopes that I had
for finding a decent solution to the *problem* ended.

BAUM: But, sir, you were not demoted after '39, you
were promoted.

EICHMANN: Forgive me, Doctor, we are talking
about power here, not rank! *Reality!* My job—and it
never changed—was evacuation and deportation:
timetables—railway time-tables! I never disposed,
assigned, never decided the fate of one man after he
reached his destination... *Ja,* I saw a few things— I
had to visit Auschwitz—and when I got back, I told
General Muller, "I can't take it. Send me to the front.
It's not in me." And I'm not the only one. That's when
the nervous breakdowns began..."Send me to the
Eastern Front", I begged Muller.

BAUM: Instead Heydrich called you in.

(Pause)

EICHMANN: May I smoke? *Gracias.* June 1941. Hitler
invaded Russia in June, and in July, Heydrich called
me in.

BAUM: Correct. Please proceed and that is as far as we
need to go, I think, in this session.

EICHMANN: *Ja,* Doctor, we will eat a hearty luncheon
today...July '41. Berlin...Heydrich says to me, "The
Fuhrer wishes...." Heydirch makes a little set speech.
"The Fuhrer wishes, the Fuhrer orders the physical
extermination of the Jews...." A long pause, silence.
I couldn't believe my ears.... The July heat, a fly

buzzing...my heart was dead. Everything was changed, from emigration to extermination. My dreams. All joy in my work was gone. My life was over!

BAUM: ...Did he use the words "Final Solution"?

EICHMANN: *Ja, ja.*

(EICHMANN *has worked himself down into a depression.* BAUM *tries to probe very gently.*)

BAUM: So... We will adjourn soon.... So, at that moment, in Heydrich's office, you knew exactly what you would be getting into.... You're very clear about that, very frank, I think, because, according to your notes, from then on "Those who were told of the Fuhrer's orders were...." —still quoting— "no longer mere bearers of orders, but were advanced to 'bearers of secrets' and they took a special oath," close quotes...I see that all this is very difficult for you.... Do you understand why—based on what you, yourself, have said, and written, why the court will make no distinction between *personal* and *legal* responsibility? And you knew. Really you knew everything, because you say the actual—

EICHMANN: *(Overlapping)* Why was I not informed that Chief Prosecutor Hausner was to be removed from my case?!

BAUM: Removed? You will have ample—

EICHMANN: *(Overlapping)* I was clearly lead to expect—

BAUM: What is the difference, Colonel? Whoever asks these questions, the *facts* remain the same.

EICHMANN: *Ja, ja,* you have the "facts" —but I have the truth.

BAUM: *(Their tones are low and charged.)* You do? And what is the truth?

EICHMANN: The truth is that, to you, I stink of corpses. Well, Herr Doctor, let me tell you that I, too, smell something in this room.

BAUM: And what is that?

EICHMANN: I smell the Eichmann-under-your-skin.... You would like to kill me, wouldn't you?

BAUM: Why do you say that?

EICHMANN: Because you believe, perhaps, that I personally murdered your entire family.

BAUM: Did you?

EICHMANN: *(In a hoarse whisper)* Whatever I have done—or you believe that I have done—I am guilty—if I am guilty at all—only in God's eyes. Remember that. Guilty only in the eyes of God!

(BAUM *and* EICHMANN *glare at each other. She reads.)*

BAUM: God? ...Yes. Quoting from your own journal: "We came to a road through a forest...a drunken captain of the local Police came to greet us...speaking in a peasant dialect. He said—

(EICHMANN's *voice and body continue the quotation, reflecting complete kinetic memory of the events.)*

EICHMANN: "The engine of a Russian submarine will be set to work and the Jews will be gassed." *Ja, ja!*... Monstrous. I vomited. To this day I cannot look at cut flesh. I could never have become a doctor. Don't talk to me about doctors! They were the worst. The camps were nothing but gigantic medical institutions. The doctors—

BAUM: *(Reads in a low, charged tone)* "They were cramming naked Jews into a large room. I refused to look inside—"

EICHMANN: No! I couldn't! I had had enough. My knees were shaking. The shrieks, the smells... It was the most horrible sight I ever....

BAUM: No, Colonel. A few months later near Minsk, you inspected a ditch that had been used for execution and then covered up and you saw, quote: "...a spring of blood gushing up from the loose earth like a fountain. And I went at once to the local S S Commander, and I said—

EICHMANN: "It is horrible what you are doing. You are turning our young men into sadists. Our youth— these farmers', and pastors' sons—will go mad. Our own boys will go mad. Slaughtering women and little children—*infants in arms*—like that!"

BAUM: "*This* was the 'most terrible thing you had ever seen in your life.'"

EICHMANN: No.

BAUM: There were worse?

EICHMANN: *Ja.*

BAUM: Where? When? ...Tell me about it?

EICHMANN: ...The tape.

BAUM: What about it?

EICHMANN: *(Whispering in her ear)* It's too personal.

BAUM: The tape machine must remain on at all times. However...

(BAUM walks down right and beckons to EICHMANN to join her. They speak in confidential tones.)

BAUM: You have some memory that is, ah...?

EICHMANN: *Ja, ja... (Pause)*

BAUM: Well, we don't have to, ah...we could come back to it later—

EICHMANN: *(Almost in her ear)* Treblinka. Treblinka was the worst. The place was transformed. It had been made to look like a perfectly ordinary railway station anywhere in Germany. The buildings, the signs, the clocks ticking—a perfect simulation: *trompe l'oeil.* And there in the middle of the station—but completely out of place like a nightmare—sits the doctor, directing people to "right" and "left"....

BAUM: Tell me about him.

EICHMANN: ..."Left, left, left. Right, right. Left, left, left..."

BAUM: Take your time, have some water. Tell me more about this nightmare. It might help.

(Pause)

EICHMANN: *Ja,* it might help.

(Pause)

BAUM: ...Why does the doctor, in the dream, terrify you so?

EICHMANN: Uh... He is, you know, in charge....

BAUM: Where are you standing in this scene? Do you see yourself?

(Pause)

EICHMANN: ...No... *(He laughs heartily.)* Ah, forgive me, I'm a bad patient. I can give you answers, but what you want are the answers *beneath* the answers, *ja?*

BAUM: Can you see the doctor's face? ...No... Is that too frightening? Let me ask you this: Are you the doctor, in the nightmare.

EICHMANN: No, just the opposite.

BAUM: What do you mean?

(Pause, then EICHMANN *shrugs.)*

EICHMANN: ...*Quien sabe? (Pause)* Maybe the doctor was God, Doctor. *(He smiles.)* And the station was Germany—

BAUM: Very interesting.

EICHMANN: *Ja*, the extermination camp was the *war*. That's it!

BAUM: Wait, I don't understand. The camp—

EICHMANN: *(Overlapping)* The camp *was* the *war*. We were all supposed to die... The next war everyone *will* die—the doctor will direct us all to the right.

(Pause)

BAUM: I see.

EICHMANN: Well... Now, I'm depressed... *(He leans over in a parody of intimacy.)* You could use my dream against me, *ja?* Your name isn't "Baum", is it? You are a great doctor, aren't you? ...So let me tell you what the nightmare really means.... *Ja*: the mid-Eastern food doesn't agree with me... *(He burps silently, then chuckles.) Ja*, now we go back to work, Professor.

BAUM: If you insist.

(BAUM hands EICHMANN a document.)

EICHMANN: This document is not correct. It is not acceptable.

BAUM: No? Why not?

EICHMANN: See? No stamp; no seal; no serial number; *and* no initials.

(BAUM stares, then laughs, as does EICHMANN.)

BAUM: Ahh, Colonel, Colonel... Well, let's forget all these pieces of paper...I wonder if you would.... No.

EICHMANN: What? May I be of service? *(He steps to the tape machine to see if it is malfunctioning again. It is not.)*

BAUM: Well... You see, I am a kind of psychologist—you guessed it—and I am interested in the reactions and associations of ah, historical figures, ah, men like you to ah, "stimuli".

EICHMANN: *Ja?*

BAUM: *Ja.* Why don't we look at a few slides, and—

EICHMANN: Ah, *ja, ja*—word games, slides and—

(BAUM *pulls down a screen and wheels out a slide machine.*)

EICHMANN: Let me, please. *Ja,* it's a German make. Ha! May I, please?

(BAUM *pauses, then nods.*)

EICHMANN: You sit there. *Ja,* I'll sit—now can you see from there? The lights. Ready? (*He turns off the lights.*)

BAUM: *Ja,* thank you, that's it.

(*As* BAUM *signals "next",* EICHMANN *presses the slide button. There are four slides. Three picture the countryside around the prisoner's boyhood home. The fourth slide stuns him.*)

BAUM: Colonel, now just push them one after the other and say the first thing that comes to you mind. Ready?

EICHMANN: At your orders. This I enjoy.

BAUM: Begin... Just say the first—

EICHMANN: Rolfe... That was my dog when I—

BAUM: Next.

EICHMANN: *Ja.* Mother.

BAUM: Next.

EICHMANN: God.

(EICHMANN *pushes the next slide. Slowly, he brings it into focus. It is the picture of a boy of about ten years. A full minute of silence*)

BAUM: What is it, Colonel?

(EICHMANN *will not answer.*)

BAUM: Colonel?

EICHMANN: Where did you get that photograph?

BAUM: But that is a photograph of you, yourself, at age ten. (*She brings up a slide of* EICHMANN's *youngest son.*) And here is Haasi, your little one. He is the image of you, isn't he?

(EICHMANN *runs over and switches on the lights.*)

EICHMANN: Who are you? —I have only been here for a few days and yet you show me documents and photographs that no one else has seen, that must have taken years to collect—

BAUM: Why does this disturb you so?

EICHMANN: (*Overlapping*) Years!... How would you have known that one day I would actually be here to see them? (*Pause*) Now it is you, Doctor, who refuses to answer. Either you are an official interrogator or you are not! And if you are not—then I expect to be paid for my time! How do you dare to treat me like some laboratory animal?

BAUM: Please, sir, you are overreacting.

EICHMANN: Now, I demand that you stop this provocation, once and for all, and resume a decent and proper course of questioning—or I shall refuse any further cooperation with your government.

(*Pause.* BAUM *begins a coldly furious cross-examination.*)

BAUM: I see.... Well... Here, sir, is the document you have rejected. It *is* a copy, but it is a *true* copy of a November 6, 1942, request for skeletons of, quote, "Jewish Bolsheviki types for scientific research." Do you remember receiving this?

EICHMANN: What?

BAUM: Living people are to be transformed into skeletons for the University of Strasbourg.

EICHMANN: It passed across my desk, but I only—

BAUM: "Transported" —yes, I know. —What's meant by page nine, here? "Most of the Jews in Area C will undoubtedly be eliminated by 'normal attenuation.'" What, sir, is "normal"?

EICHMANN: Normal dying. Old age, or heart failure—

BAUM: Or worked to death?

EICHMANN: *Ja.*

BAUM: What does "Natural Selection" mean?

EICHMANN: That comes from Himmler. Natural selection, that was his hobby.

BAUM: *(Overlapping)* But what does it mean, here?

EICHMANN: Killed, killed—what else? —Killed!

BAUM: "—the majority of the Jews will be unfit for labor." What is being suggested here?

EICHMANN: *That they should be killed!* —Wait! I will answer every question. I am ready for punishment. I am not without courage.

BAUM: *(Softly)* Then why not admit your role in what was done, and we'll say no more about it, today... *(Pause)* Colonel, you expected someone to march in here and call you a monster, to torture you, to try you, and then to hang you. Instead, I am talking to you—as one human being to another.

EICHMANN: No. You are treating me as what I am, and I make no complaint about that.

BAUM: What are you?

EICHMANN: Your prisoner... Once upon a time, I would have been *your* jailer—and I would have handled you exactly as you are handling me, here, today.

BAUM: I see. So we are the same?

EICHMANN: We are twins, Professor—whatever your name really is. And I have a shock for you. *(He pulls out a "hidden" document.)* I quote: "The Irgun Zvai Leumi" —Begin, Shamir, the Stern Gang— "in Palestine is well acquainted" —I'm still quoting, Doctor— "with the good will of the German Reich towards Zionist emigration plans"—

BAUM: Colonel, you cannot pull your irons out of the fire by quoting Stern Gang thugs to me—

EICHMANN: Quoting! —"We (the Zionists) are closely related to the totalitarian movements of Europe and its ideology and structure." Close quotes.

BAUM: A small fringe group of gangsters who have nothing to do with the State of Israel!

EICHMANN: And this will destroy you: "January, 1941. We (the Irgun)" —read it with me— "offer to take part in the war on Germany's side. This would extraordinarily strengthen the moral bases of the New Order in the eyes of all humanity."...close quotes.

BAUM: Shut your mouth!

EICHMANN: Patriots and *Policemen*! Twins.

(Pause)

BAUM: You make no distinction whatsoever between—

EICHMANN: —Between Nazis and Jews? —Doctor, please, I am not a moral idiot. I am not saying that Jews now act like Nazis. I am saying that Nazis once acted like Jews: both following orders, both "chosen people," waiting for a Messiah.... But that was yesterday. Today

I am not a Nazi, I am your prisoner. And you, Doctor, are an Israeli and not a Jew!

(Pause)

BAUM: Did I hear you correctly, Colonel?

(EICHMANN *is now in his "element".)*

EICHMANN: Let me offer you water and a cigarette, now, Doctor. And if I may be permitted to use these aids, I will demonstrate precisely why I say that my position today is that of a scapegoat—a world scapegoat.

BAUM: Feel free, sir, and then we will take our noon meal.

(EICHMANN *begins a chalk-talk at the board—a perfect Prussian schoolmaster.)*

EICHMANN: Forgive me, Doctor, I will not be able to eat a bite without clarifying— Here, now, sir: Here is the Fuhrer. The Fuhrer "wishes," then we follow the chain from the Chancellory to the S S, the Security Police, to the S D: each one is under the other, and I, myself, am a the bottom—

BAUM: Colonel, sir, may I interrupt—

EICHMANN: I have the honor of pointing out to the professor that the chain-of-command, the "Order-of-Battle," if I may use that term, runs from the Fuhrer directly down to Himmler, and under him Heydrich, and under him Muller, and under him was my office—

(EICHMANN *sketches the chain of command.* BAUM *speaks with deep irony as she draws over his diagram with her own map, thus turning the figure into a rough swastika.)*

BAUM: Herr Professor—I must interrupt—thank you. Now, sir: Hitler, Himmler, Heydrich, Muller, and *you*: you five were the fingers of one fist. Your mastery extended from the Atlantic to the North Sea to the Mediterranean—

EICHMANN: *(Overlapping)* We were at war—

BAUM: You had absolute power—

EICHMANN: And in wartime you destroy your enemy.

(BAUM stops dead, then takes out several large photographs of children from death camps. Her voice is still.)

BAUM: Your "enemy." *(Pause)* You had absolute power to exterminate—*or to save*—any human being in Europe.

EICHMANN: I had the absolute power to follow orders! Those pictures are more of your cheap Rorschach tests. *(At the board)* There it is. The chain. Where am I? Can you see me? You can't see me because I am not there.

(EICHMANN is pointing to the empty square of his office. Pause. BAUM and EICHMANN stare at each other and at the photos. Then he walks away in total denial.)

(BAUM is jolted. Deliberately she takes one of the large photographs and hangs it over the board, thus covering up EICHMANN's diagram. He moves to take down the photo, but she bars his way, speaking with the most quiet intensity.)

BAUM: Your bureau, sir, was Roman Numeral IV-B-4. "Roman IV" stands for Gestapo; "4" for religion; and "B" for Jews!

EICHMANN: I was flesh and blood, not Roman numerals—

BAUM: —All camouflage. To give the illusions of a minor department—

EICHMANN: *(Overlapping)* I was one man—

BAUM: *(Overlapping)* —so that no one would know what you were doing in secret—

EICHMANN: *(Overlapping)* I was one man. I was under orders. It was not my fault that those children were Jews!

BAUM: *(Overlapping) In secret!* —In Berlin. In Paris at 72 Avenue Foch. In *secret* at the Palais de Rothschild in Vienna. At the Majestic Hotel in Budapest—

EICHMANN: *(Overlapping)* I was under orders. Orders, orders! My God, I saved thousands of Jews—*Was konnte ich tun, ich war nur ein Mann, alles was man machen konnte habe ich getan. (He sweeps the photos of the children to the floor.)*

BAUM: *(Overlapping) Setzen Sie sich. Seien Sie ruhig. Unterbrechen Sie nicht.* Sit down. Be quiet. Stop interrupting.

EICHMANN: Go ahead. Take me out and shoot me. Do it! What are you waiting for?

BAUM: Is that what you want?

(The GUARD *enters, gun drawn.)*

BAUM: The prisoner is ready for the noon meal.

EICHMANN: Please, recall, Your Honor. I could have gone to work for the Americans like all the others. Instead I came here of my own free will. I demand that you now treat me with the respect I deserve.... *Ja,* now, we eat! *(He hands over his glasses and marches out, blindfolded again.)*

BAUM: *(To the* GUARD*)* Forty-five minutes. *(She is seething with conflicted impulses. She picks up the photos of the children as she speaks into the tape machine very quietly.)* ...Mister Prime Minister, David—this is Miriam. I am alone... I allowed the prisoner to provoke me. I am very upset with myself. This man, Eichmann, is very cunning in his stupid way. He's determined to turn us into torturers and thereby exonerate himself. If we're not very careful he will bring out the worst in all of us and turn this trial into a spectacle. His plan is simplicity itself: Admit to everything, take responsibility for nothing. In place of a memory Eichmann has only *schuld, unconscious* guilt. In place of a memory the man has charts, lists, statistics and alibis...Let me breath a minute, David. *(She stares at the chalkboard.)* I am now staring at his so-called "order-of-battle." *Du nimmst sie wahr, nimmst sie der zur "Warheit".* That's what my old teacher Martin Buber would have said— "You see it and it becomes true." Oh, yes, this piece of madness was designed for the court of law. Do not ever underestimate this little man...David, for political reasons you say you can only give me one day with the prisoner—I know this and "one day is enough," as they say, but I want you to understand that if you let this lethal "bureaucrat" live, and I can get him to remember—to remember his own humanity—*then*! Instead of one more dead Nazi degenerate, we would have a living witness to confirm, once and for all time, everything that every survivor has ever cried out to a deaf world. —Eichmann they would *hear*, Eichmann they would *believe*!... So—in spite of the total bad faith of the prisoner—I must plead with you not to let Adolph Eichmann be executed. *(A long pause)* I am not speaking here just for myself or any other survivor...I am speaking, now, for the dead themselves... *(She looks around the room.)* So, David: do not be shocked by anything I may say or do when the prisoner returns. —I will do what I have to do.... *(She turns off the tape recorder. She puts on* EICHMANN's *glasses and goes to his diagram, repeating the Buber...)* "Du nimmst sie wahr, nimmst sie der zur 'Warheit.'"

*(*BAUM *continues in German as the lights fade.)*

END OF ACT ONE

ACT TWO

(Lights bump up on scene in progress. Door slams as GUARD *exits.)*

EICHMANN: Doctor. Did you eat?

BAUM: I had some tea. Have some... Please sit. *(He looks around.)*

EICHMANN: *Ja*, where?

BAUM: Here.

EICHMANN: In your chair, Professor?

BAUM: Why not?

EICHMANN: I mean, it would not be right.

BAUM: Why not? Sit in my place, and I'll sit in yours. Perhaps then we will understand each other a little better.

*(*EICHMANN *sits and looks at* BAUM. *She gives him his glasses.)*

EICHMANN: Uh, it's warm.

BAUM: Very.

EICHMANN: *Ja*, Argentina, too, but here it's, ah....

BAUM: Close.

EICHMANN: *Ja*, humid. *Muy caliente.*

BAUM: You prefer a cool climate?

EICHMANN: Oh, *ja*.

BAUM: The fruit country, do you know it?

EICHMANN: The wine country—of course—

BAUM: You do?

EICHMANN: South of Linz. We took our honeymoon there....

BAUM: So? Your wife is from—

EICHMANN: Bohemia. That was my... Are you married, Doctor?

BAUM: I'm a widow.

EICHMANN: So? And you never remarried? ...Forgive me, please, but I mean a woman with your intelligence and, ah, bearing. A brilliant mind, an important position—

BAUM: Well. It is, perhaps, a bit late to—

EICHMANN: Never! Never too late for real love. Believe me, I know.

BAUM: You do?

EICHMANN: Absolutely. Now take me: After everything I've been through, I remarried the same woman, I started a new family—my little Haasi, I love him more than life itself... You must know. You're a woman, you're a mother, aren't you?

(BAUM *smiles cryptically.*)

EICHMANN: You smile at me like the Mona Lisa.... (*Confidential, intimate*) Tell me. Your late husband. He was a professional man—have I guessed it?

BAUM: Yes.

EICHMANN: Ha! I knew it. A linguist? A student of literature? Of philosophy.

BAUM: You don't give up, do you, Colonel?

EICHMANN: Come now, I have been totally honest with you. Be fair... Tell me a little about yourself.

BAUM: Well... Do you know Heppenheim—between Frankfurt and Heidelberg?

EICHMANN: I don't think so....

BAUM: It's a quiet village, in a valley—

EICHMANN: Wait. You mean between the Rhine and the Odenwald?

BAUM: That is where I first met Martin Buber.

EICHMANN: So?

BAUM: *Ja*. Later I studied with Karl Jaspers, and Martin Heidegger in Freiberg.

EICHMANN: Heidegger!

BAUM: *Ja*. We read Aristotle.

EICHMANN: Ah, Aristotle.

BAUM: *Ja*, the *Ninth Book of Metaphysics*. We covered one-and-a-half pages in one semester. *(Pause)* There. I think that tells you everything about my background.

EICHMANN: So...ahh, this weather...

BAUM: *Ja*... Well, we were born and grew up under the northern sky.... Here it's desert....

EICHMANN: *Ja*. Full noon, exactly.

BAUM: *Ja*. Always.

(EICHMANN laughs.)

EICHMANN: *Ahfen goniff brent dos hittel.*

BAUM: Ah, your famous Yiddish!... "On a thief's head burns his hat." Is that why you're so warm—guilt?

EICHMANN: Please, Doctor, don't spoil our little chat. *Es vet helfen vi a toiten bankes!*

BAUM: That's as helpful to me as "Blood from a dead man"—is that how you feel, Colonel?

EICHMANN: Wait, wait. Feldman, the banker, told me this—have you heard it? In my office, he told me: "The Cossack asked little Moise, 'Are you a Jew?' And Moise says, 'It all depends.'" *(He laughs.)* You see, doctor, I know—you, for instance, are Jewish, but you are not a "Jew". You know what I mean? *(Laughs)*

BAUM: So you know all about me.

EICHMANN: *Ja, ja.* Except why you are here now.

BAUM: You know why I'm here.... Because you are here.

EICHMANN: ...And your late husband, he was—

BAUM: A political scientist. He was sent to Auschwitz and Mengele cut off his head for the "Racial Institute Display of 1942 in Berlin."

EICHMANN: *(Pause)* If you please, Your Honor, if we may resume...

BAUM: Certainly... Let's pick up with the Wannsee Conference, and clear up a few details from the years '32-'42.

EICHMANN: Perfect. *Ja,* let's clean it up. Here is my record of Wannsee.

BAUM: You came to Berlin in January, '42, and Heydrich told the meeting of cabinet officers, S S leaders and civil servants that the "time" had come?

EICHMANN: *Ja, ja.* He expected the greatest difficulties. But not at all. Everyone pitched in with bright ideas and in an hour it was over and we went into a delicious luncheon. Heydrich had a Hungarian cook.

BAUM: Yes, you write here, "a cozy little social gathering". And, by the end of it, your "fate was sealed as surely as any Jew in Europe." What did you mean?

EICHMANN: Not one official there—and I was the low man, taking notes, only—*not one man* raised one objection. Not one. And these were civil servants from the old Reich, not the S S, not the Party. These were bourgeois "gentlemen" who had never deigned to give my type the time of day. And here they were tripping over each other to tell us how to make ten- point-three million Jews "disappear."...I drank my fine wine and thought, "Today I am Pontius Pilate. I have no guilt. Who am I to judge? These are the powers that be and they have smiled on the entire affair."

BAUM: ...That was Wannsee. Only an hour...then luncheon and toasts.

EICHMANN: *(Sighing) Ja, ja,* Doctor...

BAUM: Three years later, six million were gone, and you—

EICHMANN: One minute later, and Europe was "Jew Free", as we put it; and the next minute I am here talking to you. And I saw it all coming the moment that I lifted my glass in that toast to "The Final Solution".

BAUM: Yes...many have said that a conspiracy must be very small for it to be kept secret, but you claim that "The Final Solution"—a vast operation— was kept hidden for years. How can this be?

EICHMANN: *(He lectures cheerfully, pacing, picking up documents.)* Doctor, Doctor. First comes the new language. You already speak it. In days gone by, people used words like "extermination" or "liquidation", but now we had "Final Solution" and "evacuation" and "special handling." You see, Doctor, those who were required to be, quote, "evacuated" to "change their residences" also required, of course, "special handling." Then, of course, there was "resettlement", and "labor in the East"—

BAUM: But you say there was no guilt, yet everything was secrecy and code language. Isn't this an admission of guilt when—

EICHMANN: Not according to Himmler. He turned everything on its head. Did you ever hear him? "Close the double doors. Top Secret..." *(He acts out Himmler's incredible speech to the S S, in Himmler's adenoidal accents. He uses his glasses to suggest Himmler's pince-nez.)*

BAUM: You have an extraordinary gift for mimicry. But you take my point? In secret, Himmler spoke the truth to the S S, I believe.

EICHMANN: *(He moves in on her with burning intensity.)* It was fantastic! "I want to talk to you, quite frankly, on a very grave matter.... Now, I mean the clearing out of the Jews, the extermination of the Jewish race. To have witnessed that, to have been through it, and at the same time to have remained decent—that is what has made us hard! This is a page of glory in our history which has never been written and is never to be written."... This was my "Categorical Imperative." We were in a war to the finish. It was them or us. And we were Western Civilization. Full stop.

BAUM: *(Pause)* Western Civilization...Colonel. You murdered six million—

EICHMANN: *(Overlapping)* Not I—in the legal—

BAUM: *(Overlapping)* —Jews and roughly six million political prisoners, homosexuals, Gypsies, and if you had not been defeated, you contemplated the further murder of whole populations in the East. In short: genocide.

EICHMANN: And that is why, Your Honor, I would suggest that there should be an international tribunal concerning the human race—

BAUM: Pardon me, sir.

EICHMANN: —of which the Jews are merely—

BAUM: I agree with you completely but let us not become carried away again about what cannot be discussed. You are here. I am not charging you with what *would* have happened. I am simply trying to find out at what point you would have said "no." Six million, twelve million—not enough? —Twenty-five, fifty million?

EICHMANN: I understand you, Professor. Where does it end?

(They stare.)

ECHMANN: I accepted the order to transport every Jew in the world...rich, poor, famous—all. Everyone else made exceptions for their Jews—even the Fuhrer, but not me! I was an idealist! I worked with total dedication. I was the right man in the right place at the right time! At the end, Himmler ordered camps shut down. He wanted Jews to trade to the allies—"Put them in hotels—give me famous Jews to impress Roosevelt before the Russians arrive to boil us in oil." That's how they talked—but I said that I would kill Albert Einstein and Sigmund Freud before I would let them touch any little Siggy Katz!

BAUM: With you, it was all or nothing. Either an order is true or it's not, correct? No exceptions!

EICHMANN: Exactly!

BAUM: I congratulate you on also being an Aristotelian: "A thing is either true or it isn't."

EICHMANN: *Ja!* ...We believed that then, but now we see, of course, how the intellectuals poisoned our thoughts.

BAUM: And Hitler? Did they poison his thoughts, too?

EICHMANN: *Ja.* They drove him mad. That's why we pitied him.

BAUM: You pitied Adolph Hitler?

EICHMANN: We built him up, we made him God, then his luck turned bad and he couldn't do anything right. But, you know, that's war—

BAUM: Please, what were the acts of "war" committed by the Jewish people against you? I am interested.

EICHMANN: According to Berlin, the Jews were the lifeblood of both Bolshevism and Plutocracy.

BAUM: But you knew that was not true.

EICHMANN: There is only one Rothschild, *ja.* I learned that when it was too late.

BAUM: Hitler invented the modern Jew—who was both sub-human and super-human.

EICHMANN: *Ja.*

BAUM: But you didn't really believe that, did you?

EICHMANN: Of course not. Two of my mistresses were Jewesses. My step-mother's family had Jews.

(*His tone is chauvinistically confidential.* BAUM, *too, lowers her voice.*)

BAUM: And didn't Hitler tell Hess that he was the grandson of a Rothschild?

(EICHMANN *roars with laughter.* BAUM *urges him on.*)

EICHMANN: Ah, ha... Ah, Hitler... My final word on Hitler is this. He may have been wrong all down the line, but one thing is beyond dispute: the man was able to work his way up from Lance Corporal in the German Army to become Fuhrer of a people of eighty million! Of course I would have followed him anywhere—the man talked his way from the gutter to the *Arc de Triomphe.* The man made history with his mouth! I was a salesman, too, so I bought. I *bought*! I bought Hitler and I sold myself. Done and done!

BAUM: The first time you ever heard Hitler speak—can you remember it?

(EICHMANN *leaps into the role.*)

EICHMANN: As if it were yesterday: "The soil of the Fatherland will yield up crops of children and roses. But the soil must be nourished with blood, and with blood, and with blood!" I saw Communists, swept away by the sheer power, who joined the Party on the spot!

BAUM: *(Pause)* Like a God?

EICHMANN: *Ja.*

(Pause)

BAUM: And in private?

EICHMANN: In private, he was a different man. He could be thoughtful, almost gentle. He would remember your name, take your arm— a *mentsch*. And he *was* a good draftsman—and he could be witty. Once I heard him say, "A dog is a man's best friend...." *(He pretends to call a dog.)*

BAUM: Wait. This was a man who lived in Vienna like a tramp. And you—

EICHMANN: *Ja,* I know everything from Heydrich. He swore that Hitler was a Bohemian street character. That he lived off Jews in Vienna, lived like an animal in a men's hostel.

BAUM: Correct. A hotel that harbored certain types—

EICHMANN: *(Overlapping)* Then, later, he dresses like a dandy. Spats and a cane, thirty years out of date, and he eats pastries and squires women, starting with his own niece.

BAUM: The one who was found dead.

EICHMANN: *Ja, ja,* all three of his women were.
Heydrich said he murdered them to keep them quiet.

BAUM: About what?

EICHMANN: I don't know. He never said.

BAUM: What do you think?

EICHMANN: I have no idea.... When he liked a woman,
(Acting the role) he bowed and bent and scraped, all the
grand gestures.... *(Abruptly)* I know nothing about the
Fuhrer's private life.

BAUM: Shall I tell you about it?

EICHMANN: *Ja.* No. Wait. Don't think I'm one of those
swine like Kaltenbrunner who now blames everything
on Hitler and whines about how "I loved the Jews"
and that kind of excrement. Forgive me, Doctor—

BAUM: *(Overlapping)* Do you remember Hitler's
mother?

EICHMANN: I never heard of her.

BAUM: The Party Rules, Article 3, remember?

EICHMANN: No, Doctor.

BAUM: Article 3: "No German woman under forty-five
years of age shall be allowed to work in any Jewish
household." Why? What happens to German women
in—

EICHMANN: That's not me. Why ask me?

BAUM: *(Overlapping)* Surely, you know the story: That
Hitler's mother— a house servant—was seduced,
perhaps, by her wealthy Jewish employer?

EICHMANN: *Ja.* Or raped, Professor?

BAUM: Or raped... So that he could never be sure who his father was, or whether his own "blood" was "polluted."

EICHMANN: *Ja*. It's a wise man who knows—

BAUM: So the Fuhrer could have been; you, yourself, could have been—

EICHMANN: *Ja*, and you could have been an Aryan. Anything's possible, Doctor.

(*He chuckles. She smiles, then shifts to intense intimacy.*)

BAUM: Precisely: victims and executioners—could have been related by blood.... Can you tell me the nickname the other boys called you at secondary school? (*Long pause*) Wasn't it, "*der Kleine Jude*"?

(*Pause*)

EICHMANN: "*Der Kleine Jude*"... You knew that? ...I have developed a headache.

BAUM: So—you do feel guilt?

EICHMANN: No! Animal pity, nothing more.

BAUM: I see. Yet you Nazis went on and on keeping everything secret—

EICHMANN: Secret? Haven't you seen the S S films of Polish rabbis shoveling out latrines with their mouths? Haven't you seen—

BAUM: Yes. You secretly recorded every crime. For whose benefit? Why?

EICHMANN: Why ask me?

BAUM: Why else but out of guilt?

EICHMANN: Guilt? No. Guilt wants to hide what—

BAUM: No. Guilt wants to confess!

EICHMANN: No! I want my sons and the German youth of—

BAUM: You want *justification!*—The State of Israel is offering you justice.

EICHMANN: And you, Doctor, what are you offering me?

(Pause)

BAUM: Freedom.

EICHMANN: "Freedom"?!

BAUM: Freedom—from guilt.

EICHMANN: No, thank you! I prefer "power".

BAUM: Power? Oh, no: here it is the opposite of Berlin. Here, you can only have responsibility *without* power.

EICHMANN: And forgiveness?

(Pause)

BAUM: No. No human has the right to forgive you.

EICHMANN: No? Then what "human" has the right to judge me?

BAUM: Colonel, more than a million children are dead! We are talking, here, about crimes against children— born and unborn.

EICHMANN: Why are you so...obsessed with children? *(He is staring at photographs.)* Wait! These are your children, aren't they?

BAUM: ...Are they?

EICHMANN: *Ja.* I can tell. You can't fool me. These children are part of your own family.

BAUM: Put that photograph down. Don't touch it. Look at me. I implore you to talk to me—*seriously*—about how you came to commit crimes against humanity, so that—

EICHMANN: *(Overlapping)* "Humanity"! Ha! You mean a handful of politicians, don't you? And their policemen—all posing as human beings.

BAUM: No. I mean you. You, Adolph Eichmann, the "individual."

EICHMANN: Why should I tell you when you won't tell me who you are?

(Pause)

BAUM: Because you are my prisoner, and I order you to.

EICHMANN: Bravo! At last. You are the policeman and I am the prisoner: Power again. Now I am in your hands—at your disposal: what can I tell you about myself?

(Pause)

BAUM: Your personal history—start with your childhood.

EICHMANN: With pleasure! There we are, you see, in our petit-bourgeois bedroom suite. The Family Eichmann! "Tip toe to your window..." *Spatzieren* on Saturday nights to the movie shows: Chaplin, Rudolph Valentino. Dancing lessons. We were the last word in "Iron Cross Kitsch." Full of spit and polish. My boots were like glass!

BAUM: So...Hitler was Charlie Chaplin?

(EICHMANN danced to "Tip Toe Through the Tulips." They laugh together, singing; they find themselves dancing together for a moment, then reacting.)

BAUM: The winner of the All-Austria dancing contest! Adolph Eichmann! And your father—he would be so proud of you, ja?

(EICHMANN freezes in pain.)

EICHMANN: No. Ashamed of me. Always. Like his father, and *his* father, before him...

BAUM: Rest.

EICHMANN: My God...I was a *nebbish*, a *Pieter Shlemiel*—Karl Adolph Eichmann, son of Adolph Karl Eichmann. My father wore a white collar, silk hat, dress coat—and we were hungry!

BAUM: You were hungry—to be somebody.

(EICHMANN *nods.*)

BAUM: ...Now, we are coming to the point, Colonel, but you have to help me. I mean I understand petit-bourgeois Siegfrieds and *Kultur*-philistines. *(I'm German, too, after all.)* But how do these *poseurs*, these cannibals in evening dress become the Neanderthal men of the S S and the S A? How does the snobbery of the little man—anti-Semitism—become the "Final Solution" of genocide?

EICHMANN: *(He whispers.)* Fear!

BAUM: *(Softly)* Fear of the Jews?

EICHMANN: I'm afraid of you. —I am.

BAUM: Don't be afraid... *(In a maternal tone; she touches him.)* Let me tell you your story: Little Adolph, born without a brown shirt on his back, is looking for a protector. And there he is—big Adolph. And there you are marching behind him, your boots glinting in the brilliant sun of National Socialism: Big Adolph and Little Adolph!

EICHMANN: *Ja*, that's it!

BAUM: *Ja*. You knew that you were not "blond beasts" or Wagnerian Siegfrieds. You knew who you were: Slow boys at school, sly boys at home. You grew up to be non-entities, corporals, salesmen on a draw, *lumpenproletariat* scum looking for a parade—all of you, and you knew it...*Adolph Hitler was Germany and Germany was Adolph Hitler!* Isn't that true?

EICHMANN: My God! You're a prophet.

(BAUM *begins to hum softly the Horst Wessel song, and to sketch Rorschach-like designs on the whiteboard.*)

(*The Rorschach is, finally, composed of* EICHMANN's *"Chain-of-Command" diagrams from the previous session.*)

BAUM: Adolph—may I call you Adolph? —Let me continue the story of Big Adolph and Little Adolph. May I?

EICHMANN: *Ja*, please.

BAUM: While Little Adolph is in the provinces selling vacuum oil— Big Adolph is in Vienna, sleeping in the filth of a certain hotel. Already his eyes burn with a hypnotic glow—

EICHMANN: *Ja.*

(BAUM *removes his glasses gently.* EICHMANN *is falling under her spell.*)

BAUM: Yes, Belledonna. But, in reality, he was thinking about the plump peasant girls when they bend down in the fields. What a man... Then, Big Adolph goes to the front where he kills Frenchmen and washes his officer's linen.... Then, the war is over and he is talking to the little men in the street. Men like your father— like you. And you began to feel alive!

EICHMANN: *Ja!* How can you know everything?

(BAUM *softly sings the "Horst Wessell" song.* EICHMANN *begins to tap his toe. Then:*)

BAUM: I was there.... And I "know" about Hitler too.

EICHMANN: You do?

BAUM: *Ja.* The padded uniforms to hide the hollow chest. The Fuhrer reviews the troops, his arm erect and rigid for hours at a time. What a man! Except the arm is a clever prop. A dummy arm... Look, see how it comes out. See how it comes together?

(BAUM *has completed her diagram and her Rorschach. She colors in the Gestalt, now. It is a series of swastikas and yet something else.* EICHMANN *is under her spell.*)

BAUM: You see, this is Geli, his niece, or poor Magda the film star. —And here he is at the bottom, where you were—

EICHMANN: *Ja.*

BAUM: Here he is, see, our great leader; the father of our country—your father.... Come closer, Adoph, behold your father Adolph! ...Adolph Hitler lies here, "under," so that the woman, here, "over," can defecate and urinate on him...Then, later, he kills them so no one will ever know....

(EICHMANN *stares, paralyzed, at the drawing.*)

BAUM: *"Nascimur in faecibus et urina."* We are born among feces and urine.

(EICHMANN *starts to mumble to himself.* BAUM *grips him, as he sits, by the shoulders. He stares up at her.*)

EICHMANN: Hitler...Himmler...Heydrich...Muller...me...

BAUM: *(Overlapping)* We're born among it, and in the camps they died among it. They did it to him, he did it to you, and you did it to twelve million. Flesh and blood. Feces and urine. That's your *"Fuhrerprinziple."* The ovens and vans were covered with excrement every time, weren't they? We're all *only human.* That's why it is necessary, now, for one man to stand before history and take responsibility.

(*Something deep in* EICHMANN *is stirring.* BAUM *moves in for the "kill." Both speak very softly.*)

EICHMANN: Doctor—you know—*you*, I would have saved....

BAUM: No. "No exception" —remember? ...But I can help *you*—here, today.

EICHMANN: You would save me?

BAUM: You could "save" yourself.... Do you remember that there were some few people in Germany who stood up against the Race laws?

(Pause)

EICHMANN: The "White Crows"—

BAUM: Who spoke up—

EICHMANN: And got their necks chopped off.

BAUM: Hear me: how do you want to be remembered by History—and by your sons? *(Indicates tape recorder)* A voice in the mob—or as a human being who—

EICHMANN: Who only did—

BAUM: Who took responsibility—full responsibility for his life—

EICHMANN: *Ja*—and then you hand me the key to that door there—

BAUM: I'm giving you much more: the chance to join the human race!

*(*EICHMANN *laughs, then cries and rages, throwing chairs. The* GUARD *runs in,* BAUM *waves him out.)*

EICHMANN: I join nothing anymore! Why can't I make you understand: I had only the power to do it—never to *stop* it! —Now I will tell you your story: It's *you* who feel guilty! Not me. *You!* Because you're *alive*. That's your guilt. I'm a dead man, but you're *alive*. And that's your secret!

BAUM: It is?

EICHMANN: *Ja, ja.* You want to bring the children back to life. But you can't—so kill yourself. Have the courage to kill yourself—

(BAUM *stalks* EICHMANN *now, and he twists and turns about the room.)*

BAUM: Like you?! You arranged your own arrest, didn't you?

EICHMANN: "Arranged"?

BAUM: Of course. I know your secret, Adolph. You *wanted* to be captured—

EICHMANN: *(Overlapping)* No, you're—

BAUM: *(Overlapping)* To be brought here, to be executed—

EICHMANN: You *do* think I'm mad—

BAUM: I know that you are not mad! You came here to die. Because you *do* feel guilt-because-you-are-a-human-being.

EICHMANN: I-am-not-a-human-being!

BAUM: You are—and I will prove it to you: You sent your wife back to Germany to attend a funeral; you gave your real name to a Dutch journalist—here are the documents!; you took a public bus to work every day.

EICHMANN: I had to work!

BAUM: No! You did not have to. You could have lived in magnificent isolation like Mengele! You did not slip away after the war like a "bit player." You were transported along the Odessa Route, the "Monastery Route" —the royal road from Rome to Rio—courtesy of the Vatican. You were, Colonel, a very important war criminal. The other Nazis gave *you* "special handling" —orchestrating your escape to Latin America. But you couldn't stand it, could you? No mention of Adolph Eichmann in the history books. So you took the road that has led you from oblivion, here to the foot of the gallows and History. Admit it, now sir! *(She pulls out photographs.)* Here are photographs of you standing in front of the Israeli Embassy in Buenos Aires. Do you deny it? Look at—

(EICHMANN *rips away the photos. He is hysterical.)*

EICHMANN: You have all the answers. There is nothing left but to shoot me with that gun there, and that will be the "Final Solution" to the "German Problem." *(He has torn up a handful of documents and photos and begins to set them on fire in the ashtray.)*

BAUM: Shall I?

EICHMANN: *Do it!* And I will jump into my grave happy. And my last request is that you take my ashes to Auschwitz and mingle them with the children's. There, right there, plant orchards and stands of trees of every kind—make that desert bloom! So go now to Auschwitz, *Anus Mundi,* to the asshole of the world, and plant trees, and *I will do whatever you say!*... You think I'm mad! Of course! Doesn't that prove I'm like everybody else? Ha! The madman speaks Hegel to the Professor Doctor.

BAUM: You are not mad, Colonel.

EICHMANN: You want me to be the King of the Jews— *again*! Why not? Israel, the world, the dead children— who else, the Martians? —now need Adolph Eichmann to crucify himself legally.

BAUM: Stop it! ...Stop quoting Jesus, it's bad for the nerves.... Look at me, Adolph.

(EICHMANN *runs away, afraid of being hypnotized again.)*

EICHMANN: Liar! Jew! Whore! Jew! Jew! Jew! Pay me, Jew! You and your filthy Jewish science—your psychology. You want to write a book about me, you want to dine out on Adolph Eichmann? Write this:

"I will jump into my grave laughing because I killed every Jew in the world!" I came here to write a book about it—with you! You can be my ghost writer! *(He screams with laughter.)* My ghost writer—my ghost!

(BAUM's voice and gestures stop EICHMANN's fit.)

BAUM: Look at these faces. *(Photos of the children)* The names and dates are gone: these are your ghosts...but something is bleeding through—don't you feel it? *(Her voice shakes.)* Something?

EICHMANN: I cannot stand this torture anymore! Don't blame me—blame *God*! It was fated—*behfele*.

BAUM: God is not here, sir, to answer for his crimes, but you are.

EICHMANN: No, God is not here. And God was not *there*! When I transported the children, I tried to force *Him* to break *His* silence. I dared Him!

BAUM: So there's no God. There's only you.

EICHMANN: No God...so man is shit!

BAUM: Is that your last word, Colonel?

EICHMANN: That's it, Doctor: No God—and no History, either. Don't you see: anyone could have been me. Whether Adolph Eichmann said "yes" or "no" would not have changed the fate of a single person.

BAUM: Yes, it would—

EICHMANN: No, it would not! —It was all bad luck, don't you see.... I wanted to ride on Himmler's running board; it was all a mistake.... It was not a question of monsters or men, Doctor. We were all—we *are* all monsters, who've been called "Human Beings" too soon... Now, I want my tea!

(BAUM and EICHMANN stare at each other, drained. Then, slowly, she turns off the recorder. He whispers in panic.)

EICHMANN: What do you think you're doing? Turn it on!

BAUM: No more orders, Colonel.

(BAUM *slowly takes off her holster.* EICHMANN*'s voice is a hoarse whisper now.)*

EICHMANN: A policeman who does not follow orders....

BAUM: ...is not a policeman?

EICHMANN: Then who are you?

BAUM: No more orders. And it was never loaded.... We are off the record, now. Officially, I stand before you naked, and there are just the two of us.

EICHMANN: *(Whispering)* Who are you?

BAUM: This is your last chance, Adolph Eichmann. Violate your orders, for *once*, and you *will* save your sons, and mine.

EICHMANN: They are your children. Admit it!

BAUM: *(Pause)* Yes.

EICHMANN: I knew it!

BAUM: They're my brother's....

EICHMANN: What?

BAUM: And his brother's...Colonel, the truth is: following orders could change even Jews into executioners. *And that must never happen!* And that is why I am breaking my orders.

EICHMANN: You know your *Talmud*, Professor: "What *has* happened, *will* happen."

BAUM: No. If we break our orders—there can be new life. *(Searching)* In Poland where the death camps were—*blawatski* is blooming, tiny blue flowers; and lilacs at Auschwitz—and in you a soul!

EICHMANN: *Ja,* all that is a dream of the nursery, Doctor.... Now turn that machine on.

(BAUM*'s response continues low and intimate, drilling into* EICHMANN.)

BAUM: No. You and I are both going to break our orders now, and enter the world hidden under these mountains of documents. Take my hand... Take it—I'm coming with you.

EICHMANN: *(Trying to break her spell, running to the door.)* No! This is provocation. Your orders are to pretend that you are not following orders. I know every trick. *Don't touch me!* Please, *Ich habe* hunger.

BAUM: Adolph—

EICHMANN: *Sieg Heil!* Torturer! —I am not free—I never was! And you are not free—

BAUM: I-am-*not*-following-orders—

EICHMANN: You are: You may not think so but you are! We all are!

(BAUM *starts to tear up documents.*)

EICHMANN: What are you doing?

BAUM: Look, Adolph—I am not following orders.

EICHMANN: No—don't.

BAUM: I am not following orders.

EICHMANN: If you rip these up...that's my defense!

BAUM: No—it's your indictment. *(She continues littering the floor with documents and ripping them up.)*

EICHMANN: You cannot destroy the record. You cannot tear up the past.

BAUM: *(Overlapping)* I am not—not—not following orders! There. Now I am a criminal, too.

EICHMANN: They will hang you for this. *(Pause)* You would do this for me? —Why? —You're shaking.... Now you're terrified, too.

BAUM: Yes, I'm shivering. Because it's cold here, in this open station—what's that music? Stay with me. Don't leave me here alone.

(BAUM and EICHMANN are moving together.)

BAUM: I see it: Do you see it—do you hear it—the trains, the doctors, the dogs, the guards, the clock ticking—twelve noon—and there: here they come, the children first—the mothers, the grandparents, and the band is playing. *(She hums.)* And here you are! And you bend and you touch a child's head—

EICHMANN: *(His head is against her breast.)* I can't.

BAUM: You *can.* You can be the "White Crow."

EICHMANN: The White Crow... *(He lifts his arms. Takes a step. His pants fall down.)*

BAUM: Look straight into the sun. You see them. The faces. Behind the numbers—the faces—*ja, ja.* Now, we tear our garments— *(She tears his pockets and smears his face with cigarette ashes, and her own, as well.)* —you know the orthodox ritual—we smear ourselves. Kneel down—speak to your victims. Speak to them. Have pity on them—*Rachmones! (She tries to force him down.)* See how they run from the soldiers. Save them! Save them, Adolph. Break your orders! Break your chains. Break them now!

EICHMANN: I can't. *(He trembles, mumbling, unable to take the first step.)*

BAUM: I order you to remember! Look, look at me! Remember. You were there. I was there. I know everything. You were there! *(In desperation, she acts out the role of the younger Nazi EICHMANN, using the tape machine as a P A system. As EICHMANN)* "Left, right, left,

right. *Juden*, march. *Links, zwei, drei, vier. Juden*, soon
you will be safe in the East. *Links, zwei, drei, vier." (She
seizes him.)* "You, *schnell*, hurry. You'll miss your train.
Achtung! Achtung! This is Colonel Eichmann speaking.
This is *obersturmbannfuhrer* Eichmann. Let the band
play. Jews, march! *Juden raus, raus, raus, Juden raus!"*

EICHMANN: No...no...please, no...

BAUM: You little Jew, get on that train.

(BAUM *beats* EICHMANN *with the gunbelt. He strains
at his invisible bonds like a twisted Titan. The whipping
continues.)*

BAUM: *Kleine Jude!* Break your orders. Break your
chains. Kleine Jude. Kleine Jude.

EICHMANN: *(Panting)* I can't—I can't—I can't.

BAUM: Wait, who is that child? Who are you? What's
your name?

(BAUM *hits the slide projector, bringing up the image of*
EICHMANN's *son.)*

EICHMANN: Haasi!

BAUM: Throw him in with the others. —Close the
doors!

EICHMANN: Haasi, Haasi! No!

BAUM: Now, will you do it?! —Will you stop it?!

(BAUM *puts the microphone almost in* EICHMANN's *mouth.
He gags and cannot "stop" the train. —We hear his hoarse
panting... She is in a state of suspended anguish; slowly she
picks up the gun belt. Her voice is low and building.)*

BAUM: Do it. You have to do it.... For your son, for all
the children... What did they feel? *(She beats him.)* The
children—what did they feel? *(Beats him)* When the
ovens closed on them—the children—what did they
feel? *(Beats him)* The pain! The pain that filled up the

world! When they climbed over each other toward the hole in the ceiling—what did they think, what did they *feel*? *(Beats him)* ...Claw marks up the walls—on the *ceiling!* —Do you know what they felt—the old people—the *children*— what did they *feel—feel—feel!*

(BAUM and EICHMANN both collapse on top of each other— exhausted, devastated. At length—)

EICHMANN: ...It's too late. I don't know how.

(Long pause, BAUM is silent.)

EICHMANN: Tell me what to do.

(BAUM stares at EICHMANN. Silence)

EICHMANN: You cannot help me—can you? —And our suffering will never end. (Pause. He rises, salutes, tries to click his heels, limps to the door, stamps his foot.

(The GUARD enters and starts to blindfold EICHMANN. BAUM takes the blindfold away, clutching it.)

(Finally EICHMANN shuts his own eyes and exits.)

BAUM: *(To herself, at length)* You would do it for Hitler. You would do it for me....

(BAUM, alone, goes to the tape. She is unable to speak. She turns off the tape, then rewinds it and plays a small section of EICHMANN speaking. She rewinds and repeats.)

(EICHMANN's voice fills the room.... Then, BAUM turns the machine off, takes in the room and what has happened. She leaves.)

(Through the window bars—a red sun)

END OF PLAY